1

The Healing Blueprint™
First Edition, 2025
ISBN: 979-8-9991205-1-9

Published by **ENAM + SoulSpace**
Boynton Beach, Florida

This book is a work of nonfiction based on personal experience, professional insight, and researched information. While every effort has been made to ensure accuracy, the author and publisher assume no responsibility for errors or omissions. This content is not intended as medical, psychological, or legal advice and should not replace guidance from a licensed professional.

Cover design and interior layout by Evelyn Wiggins
Printed in the United States of America

For more resources, visit: https://evelynwiggins.podia.com

Table of Contents

Before you begin, pause.

Listen.

Can you feel it?

That tiny ache you have been ignoring when you walk into certain rooms...

The tension you carry when you step through your own doorway...

The urge to exhale, but not knowing where to place your breath...

It is not just in your body.

It is in your space.

And it has been calling you home.

This is not just a book.

This is a threshold.

A rabbit hole.

A return.

Because the truth is, we do not just live in homes.

We live inside memories.

Inside meaning.

Inside the energy of who we were... and who we are still becoming.

What if I told you your home is speaking? What if the clutter is grief?

The dim lighting is exhaustion? The unused corner is the part of you that still has not healed?

This is not about paint colors and throw pillows.

This is about waking up the spirit of your space.

So, I ask you gently, but seriously:

Are you willing to go there?

To walk into each room with new eyes?

To touch the walls like they hold prayers?

Because once you begin, you cannot unsee it.

Once you decide to feel, *really* feel what your space has absorbed...

You start a chain reaction.

You begin to reclaim.

Not just your style.

Not just your peace.

But your presence.

This is not an ordinary book.

It is not a trend.

It is not a fix.

It is a portal.

You will leave this experience different than you entered.

More whole.

More aware.

More home within yourself than ever before.

So, open the window.

Light the candle.

Turn the page.

The journey has already begun.

And the space you have been craving is waiting.

Welcome to The Healing Blueprint.

Let us go deeper.

SECTION 01: The SoulSpace™ Method

"A Design Philosophy for the Healing Era"

There is a difference between *decorating* a home and *reclaiming* a sanctuary.

The SoulSpace™ Method is not a style trend or aesthetic guide.

It is a healing philosophy.

A way of coming home to yourself regardless of your background, gender, or belief system.

This method was born not from theory, but from experience.

It came to life in moments of silence, stillness, and survival.

Moments when I, like so many of us, needed my space to hold me while I healed.

What I have created here is for everyone.

Whether you are anchored in faith, guided by energy, moved by science, or somewhere in-between.

Because no matter who you are, you deserve peace.

You deserve safety.

You deserve a home that feels like belonging.

The SoulSpace™ Method is built on **four foundational pillars**:

They are not rules.

They are invitations, doorways to realignment.

Anchors to help you design your space as a sacred partner in your healing.

1. Stillness

Your nervous system deserves calm.

This pillar centers on quieting the noise: visually, emotionally, and energetically.

Stillness in design is not emptiness.

It's clarity. Breathing room. A sense of enoughness.

Research shows that visual clutter increases cortisol, the stress hormone, leading to anxiety, overwhelm, and even decision fatigue (Princeton Neuroscience Institute, 2011).

Stillness tells your body: "You can *exhale* now."

2. Style

Your beauty is not a trend; it is a truth.

Your space should reflect you. Not a Pinterest board. Not a minimalist checklist. Not what's "in."

Style is the emotional fingerprint of your surroundings.

It is the small moments of self-expression that say,

"I see myself here. I am allowed to take up space."

It does not matter if your style is bold, earthy, soft, spiritual, luxurious, or nostalgic.

What matters is that it is *yours*.

3. Spirit

Your space holds energy. Clear it with care.

Whether you call it energy, the Holy Spirit, the atmosphere, or vibration, every space carries a charge.

You do not have to be "woo" to feel it.

Have you ever walked into a room after an argument? The tension?

Palpable.

That is the invisible weight about which we are talking.

This pillar invites you to be intentional with what lingers:

Light a candle.

Say a prayer.

Open a window.

Burn herbs.

Play worship music.

Speak life into the room.

Choose the practices that align with your belief system.
What matters is the clearing, not the label you give it.

4. Story

Your home should grow with you.
You are not who you were five years ago.
Your space should not be either.

Your rooms hold echoes of old versions of you, some still
healing, some already gone.

This pillar is about letting go of what no longer reflects who you are becoming.

Reclaim your corners.

Redefine your energy.

Tell a new story through your surroundings.

This is the SoulSpace™ Method.

It is inclusive. It is accessible. It is deeply human.

It is a framework you can layer with your rituals, your faith, your science, your softness.

And it always begins with this question:

What if your space could help you heal?

SECTION 02: The Self-Healing Space Audit

"What Is Your Home Trying to Tell You?"

Let us pause here.

Not to change anything yet, but to listen.

Because before you can reclaim your space,

You must understand what it has been holding.

This is not about "fixing" your home.

This is about *feeling* it.

Because every space you enter is speaking to you.

And if you are quiet long enough, your home will tell you the truth.

So, let us walk through it room by room, breath by breath, and begin the Self-Healing Space Audit.

Start Here: Slow Down.

Do not rush this part.

You do not need tools or timers.

You just need presence.

Stand in each room and ask:

What part of me lives here?

What memories live in this room?

What do I avoid looking at or dealing with in this space?

Does this room reflect who I am now, or a version of me I have outgrown?

Let yourself answer honestly.

Let yourself feel uncomfortable if it comes.

You are not here to judge.

You are here to observe and reclaim.

Let Us Go Deeper: Sensory Check-In...

Ask yourself:

What smells are present? Are they grounding or heavy?

What lighting exists? Is it nurturing or draining?

What textures are around you? Are they comforting or forgotten?

What sounds fill this space? Is it silence, chaos, or peace?

What emotions rise when I sit here alone?

Each sense is a language your space uses to speak back.

Emotional Inventory:

Write these down or sit with them as reflection prompts:

Which room makes you feel most at home in your body?

Which room do you avoid and why?

What object do you keep that you know you have outgrown?

Where in your home do you shrink yourself or disconnect?

If your home could talk, what would it ask you to release?

No Shame. Just Sacred Awareness.

This audit is not about shame.

This is data for your healing.

It is an invitation to notice without rushing to fix.

To name, without needing permission.

To remember that your space reflects your healing journey... and deserves to evolve with you.

This is sacred work.

And the moment you begin to ask better questions,

You will begin to make space for better answers.

You do not just audit a room. You awaken it.

SECTION 03: What Color Feels Like

"The Energetics of Color, Design, and Emotional Memory"

Before you ever say a word, your space is already speaking.

And one of the most powerful languages it speaks in… is **color.**

Color is more than aesthetic, it is emotional.

It is psychological.

It is spiritual.

It is ancestral.

In therapy, color is used to evoke feelings.

In spiritual practice, it is used to cleanse, energize, and protect.

In the nervous system, colors influence how safe or stimulated we feel, and even how well we sleep (National Sleep Foundation, 2021).

So, let us explore what color feels like and how to use it with intention, not just instinct.

Color Symbolism Guide: The SoulSpace Lens:

These are not rules.

They are reflections.

Use what resonates. Leave what does not.

Let this guide your room resets, mood boards, and object placement.

White:

Clarity. Light. Room to breathe.

Used to create space emotionally and visually.

In spiritual traditions, white often symbolizes purity and presence.

Use it when your spirit feels heavy, and you need a reset.

Taupe & Earth Tones:

Stability. Stillness. Grounding.

These colors calm the nervous system and encourage emotional regulation.

Use when you are trying to feel safe in your body again.

Blush & Warm Neutrals:

Tenderness. Vulnerability. Softness.

These colors support inner child healing and emotional rest.

Use in spaces where you want to feel held.

Midnight Blue:

Intuition. Wisdom. Sacred stillness.

This is a reflective color, a cue to go inward.

In Christian tradition, deep blue represents faith and divine revelation.

Use in reading nooks, meditation corners, or bedrooms.

Olive & Deep Greens:

Healing. Growth. Ancestral presence.

Green is associated with the heart chakra, restoration, and rebirth.

Use when you want to feel connected to lineage, legacy, or nature.

Burnt Orange & Copper:

Transformation. Fire. Renewal.

This color is bold, activating, and honest.

Use when you are shifting identities or walking into a new season.

Charcoal & Black Accents:

Boundaries. Depth. Mystery.

These tones ground a space, providing contrast and energetic protection.

Use with intention- too much may feel heavy, but just enough creates power.

How to Apply This:

Use color to support the function of a room (ex: calming tones in bedrooms, energizing ones in creative spaces)

Let the feeling you want lead your design, not just Pinterest inspiration.

Ask yourself:

What am I calling into this space?

And what color holds that frequency?

You do not need to redo your whole home.

You just need to choose color like you choose company: *intentionally*.

Your walls *remember*. Your eyes *absorb*.

Your space *reflects* your state.

So, speak with color.

And let your space say what your spirit needs to hear.

SECTION 04: Rituals That Reset a Room

"Clearing Energy, Creating Peace, and Claiming Your Space"

Let us start with the truth:

You do not have to be "spiritual" to sense when a room feels heavy.

You do not have to be religious to feel presence.

You do not need crystals or sage (unless you want them).

What you need is intention and authority.

This section is about reclaiming your home as a place of peace.

Clearing what you cannot see and anchoring what you want to feel.

Ritual is not just ceremony.

It is any action you take on purpose to remind your body and soul:

"This space belongs to me."

Here are 5 SoulSpace rituals that blend emotional grounding, spiritual presence, and energetic awareness. Choose what resonates. Leave what does not.

1. The Morning Touch:

For emotional presence.

Before you do anything, place your hand on the wall or door frame.

Close your eyes. Breathe.

Whisper:

"This is my space. This is my peace."

This may seem simple, but in trauma recovery and nervous system therapy, sensory grounding is one of the most powerful tools. (Somatic Experiencing Institute, 2020)

Touching your space while claiming it tells your body you are safe here.

2. Smoke & Sweep:

For energetic clearing

This can be incense, frankincense, herbs, or even Florida water in a spray bottle.

It is not about the tool; it is about the intention.

As you sweep or clear, say:

"I release what no longer serves this space."

Spiritually, this aligns with cleansing in many traditions, from Psalms anointing to indigenous smoke rituals.

Scientifically, scent-based rituals trigger memory, relaxation, and emotional release (Harvard Health, 2019).

3. The Sacred Corner:

For emotional anchoring.

Pick a neglected area of your home. Clean it.

Place something sacred there:

A candle.

A plant.

A prayer card.

A framed affirmation.

A scripture or verse.

Do not underestimate what this does to your psyche.

It is a statement that says:

"Even forgotten corners deserve intention."

(So do you.)

4. Ancestral Water:

For stillness + spiritual connection.

Place a clear bowl of water near your bed or entryway.

You do not have to call it an altar unless that aligns for you.

Water absorbs, reflects, and purifies.

In Christianity, water is baptism and cleansing.

In African spiritual systems, it is communication and reverence.

In science, it symbolizes flow and emotional regulation.

Each morning, pour the water out with thanks.

Say:

"Let what this space held be released."

5. The Mirror Blessing:

For identity and worthiness.

Look at yourself in the mirror. Not to critique, but to connect.

Say aloud:

"I am safe. I am soft. I am strong. I am worthy of beauty."

This rewires your inner narrative, especially for those healing from trauma, self-neglect, or shame.

Repeat daily until your body believes it is true.
Because eventually, it will.

A Final Word on Ritual:
Ritual does not have to be mystical.
It just has to be meaningful.

Ritual says, "This space is not just a container. It is a reflection of me. And I choose to make it sacred."

Whatever you choose, do it with intention.
And let your space remember who you are.

SECTION 05: Reflections That Move Energy

"Journaling Into the Heart of Your Space".

Before you write, breathe.

This is not a worksheet.

This is a return.

You are not just journaling.

You are witnessing your own healing.

We carry so many unsaid things.

Memories we packed into boxes.

Emotions we left behind furniture.

Versions of us are still sitting silently in corners, waiting to be released.

This space, these pages, are for them.

For you.

Light a candle if you need to.

Wrap yourself in something warm.

Let this chapter be a ceremony.

Phase One: What Has This Space Held?

Close your eyes. Walk through your home in your mind.

Now write freely in response to these prompts:

1. What room in your home carries the most emotion? Why?

2. What moment in this home changed you, and where did it happen?

3. Where do you feel the most resistance in your space? What emotion lives there?

4. Is there a part of your home you have neglected as a reflection of yourself?

5. If your home had a voice, what would it whisper to you about what you have carried?

Pause. Breathe. Let it land.

Phase Two: Reflection as Release:

Now we shift.

These prompts are not about discovery. They are about decluttering energetically.

6. Write a letter to one room in your home. Tell it what it is absorbed for you. Thank it. Forgive it. Free it.

7. List five items you've been keeping out of guilt. What would releasing them symbolize?

8. Who did you become in this space, and who are you becoming now?

9. What belief or memory do you want your home to release with you? Be specific. Burn it safely or bury it.

10. Describe, in sensory detail, the feeling of peace you want your home to carry next.

Optional Grounding Practice: The After-Journal Ritual

After writing:

Wash your hands (symbolic clearing).

Open a window or play soft music.

Speak aloud:

"I release what no longer needs to stay. This home is healing, and so am I."

Affirmation Anchor:

"I honor what this space has held. I honor who I have been. And I give myself permission to change."

SECTION 06: Affirmations That Rewire the Atmosphere

"Speaking Safety, Beauty, and Belonging into Every Room"

(Sacred Language, Everyday Practice)

Words are architecture.

Every time you speak to your space, you are either reinforcing an old blueprint or building a new one.

Affirmations are not just phrases you tape to a wall.

They are frequency shifts.

They speak to your nervous system.

To your inner child.

To your spirit.

To the quiet corners of your home that remember what you have survived.

They are not magical by themselves.

But when paired with intention and repetition, they become transformative.

So, let us design with our words now.

You can whisper them.

Speak them during your cleaning rituals.

Post them on your mirrors.

Pray them into every corner.

Make them yours.

Spoken Language, Layered Healing:

In the Black church, we call it speaking life.

In energy work, it is raising vibration.

In therapy, it is reframing belief.

In SoulSpace, we call it **atmosphere writing.**

Let us write peace into the air you breathe.

Daily SoulSpace Affirmations:

"My home reflects who I'm becoming, not who I used to be."

"I give myself permission to take up beautiful, sacred space."

"Stillness is a gift, not a problem to solve."

"This space is enough. I am enough."

"The version of me that lived in survival no longer designs this space."

"My softness is safe here."

"Everything in this room honors who I am and where I'm going."

"My presence alone makes this space sacred."

<u>Room-by-Room Affirmations:</u>

Bedroom:

"This is where I return to myself.

I am safe to rest.

I am worthy of sleep.

My dreams are protected here."

Bathroom:

"I cleanse not just my body, but my spirit.

I release what is no longer mine to carry.

I am renewed in this space."

Living Room:

"Joy lives here.

Connection lives here.

I create space for laughter, softness, and breathing room."

Kitchen:

"I nourish myself with intention.

I bless the hands that prepare.

This is a space of provision and gratitude."

Closet / Mirror Spaces:

"I am allowed to change.

I am allowed to evolve.

I do not shrink to fit this room, this room expands to reflect me."

Optional Prayer Prompt (faith-neutral):

"God, Creator, Spirit, let this space reflect Your peace.

Let it be full of what heals, emptied of what harms.

May the energy in this room rise to meet me.

May I treat it as sacred because I am sacred.

Let every corner carry clarity.

Let every object hold meaning.

And may I never forget I deserve to feel safe here."

SoulSpace Practice Tip:

Print three affirmations.

Place them where you:

Wake up.

Rest.

Avoid.

Let them become quiet teachers.

Speak to them every day for a week.

Let them teach your home a new language.

SECTION 07: The Integration

"Let the Work Sink In"

You have walked through reflection.

You have cleared energy.

You have reimagined your home as a sacred extension of self.

But do not confuse this for the end.

This is a threshold.

The space between the healing you have tasted.

and the life you are ready to embody.

You have done more than complete a book.

You have broken a cycle.

You have chosen presence over perfection.

Intention over impulse.

Sanctuary over survival.

And now?

You do not just *have* a blueprint.

You *are* one.

Your home is no longer a mirror of chaos.

It is a canvas for rebirth.

It is a place where healing happens in quiet, ordinary ways:

In the way you open the blinds before speaking to anyone

In the way you wash dishes with music playing softly

In the scent that meets you after a long day

In the prayer whispered while folding a blanket over your own shoulders

This is what sacred space feels like.

Not curated. Not filtered.

Lived. Felt. Grounded.

What You have Built:

You have created a space that...

- Holds your evolution, not your shame

- Reflects who you are, not who you have been told to be

- Protects your peace, not just your possessions

And as you move forward through this life, you now carry tools to return home to yourself, repeatedly.

Not just when you move.

Not just when it is convenient.

But whenever your spirit calls you back to the truth:

"I deserve to live in beauty. I am allowed to be held by my home."

Let this be your reminder:

You can reset whenever you need to.

You can reclaim your space at any time.

You can start again right now.

From Here Forward...

This is not goodbye.

It is grounding.

Before you move to the next practice...

Before you start the rituals, the reset, the challenge...

Let this chapter settle into your bones.

Let it say:

"You did this. You are doing this. You *are* this."

Healing is no longer something you chase.

It is something you live in.

Welcome home.

SECTION 08: Soulful Design in Action

"Textures, Lighting, Plants & the Ritual of Beautiful Living"

You have done the deep work.

You have reflected, released, spoken life into your space.

Now it is time to bring it all together visually, emotionally, and energetically.

Because a healing space is not just about what it feels like emotionally.

It is also about what it holds physically.

This chapter is about the tangible tools of SoulSpace:

Textures. Lighting. Plants. Scent. Style.

What's trending? What is timeless?

What works scientifically, spiritually, and soulfully.

Whether you live in a high-rise apartment, a tiny house, a bedroom you rent, or your forever home, these principles apply to you.

01. Texture: The Quietest Language of Healing:

Why it matters:

Texture affects how your body responds to space, whether you lean in or pull away.

Scientific note:

Soft, natural materials can lower cortisol and stimulate serotonin (British Journal of Psychology, 2018).

SoulSpace design tip: Layer three textures per room.

This adds depth, comfort, and warmth without needing "more stuff."

Try this:

Linen curtains for breathability.

Woven baskets for storage (and ancestral memory).

Velvet pillows or boucle throws for sensual softness.

Raw wood or cane pieces for grounding.

Reflection Prompt:

Where in your life could softness replace survival? Add that texture to your space.

02. Lighting: Mood Medicine for the Mind & Spirit:

Why it matters:

Light shifts the mood of a space instantly.

Harsh lighting overstimulates the nervous system.

Warm lighting soothes it.

Scientific note:

Cool light boosts alertness, but warm-toned light increases melatonin and supports rest (Lighting Research Center, 2019).

SoulSpace design tip:

Every room should have three layers of lighting:

Ambient (main light source).

Task (lamps, sconces).

Accent (candles, LED glow, fairy lights).

Try this:

Salt lamps for grounding glow.

Dimmer bulbs to adjust intensity.

Curtain sheers to soften natural light.

Clip-on spotlights for targeted peace.

Reflection Prompt:

Is your space helping you rest, or keeping you wired? Adjust lighting accordingly.

03. Plants: Living Symbols of Growth:

Why it matters:

Plants are not just décor. They are companions in healing.

They improve air quality, increase serotonin, and reduce stress (NASA Clean Air Study, 1989 + Journal of Physiological Anthropology, 2015).

SoulSpace design tip:

Start with 1–2 easy-care plants, especially if you're new to it.

Try this:

Snake Plant (cleans air, low maintenance).

Pothos (trailing energy, ancestral flow).

Lavender (scent + peace).

Peace Lily (hello... name says it all).

Reflection Prompt:

What do you want to grow within yourself? Mirror it in the plant you choose.

04. Aromatherapy: Scent as Sacred Memory:

Why it matters:

Scent bypasses logic and goes straight to the limbic brain, your emotional control center.

Scientific note:

Lavender and rosemary improve memory and reduce anxiety (National Institutes of Health, 2020).

SoulSpace scent guide:

Lavender: calming, anxiety relief.

Frankincense: spiritual grounding.

Citrus: energy, joy.

Eucalyptus: mental clarity, breath.

Sandalwood: peace, emotional release.

Try this:

Oil diffusers.

Soy candles.

Simmer pots (lemon, cinnamon, herbs).

Spritz bottles with essential oil + witch hazel.

Reflection Prompt:

What emotion do you want your space to evoke when you walk in? Let scent hold that vibration.

05. What's Trending (That Actually Works):

This book is timeless. But here are a few design shifts happening now that align with the SoulSpace™ philosophy:

Sculptural candles & ceramics: Imperfect beauty.

Earth-tone walls: Deep grounding (clay, ochre, sage).

Quiet luxury textures: Plush, layered softness with restraint.

Wellness corners: Intentional chair + candle + tray setups.

Statement mirrors: Identity meets energy expansion.

Oversized art: Let one piece carry emotion instead of over-decorating.

These trends work because they are not about excess, they're about intention and presence.

06. Where to Shop (Budget-Friendly + Soul-Aligned):

You do not need to break the bank to create healing space. Try:

IKEA: basic neutral furniture + lighting.

H&M Home / Zara Home: high-style accents, textiles.

Etsy: handmade ceramics, affirmation art, incense.

Thrift Stores + Estate Sales: vintage soul, natural patina.

Amazon: (search: organic bedding, handmade planters, LED warm bulbs).

Reflection Prompt:

Instead of buying more, what can you reframe, relocate, or repurpose with intention?

SoulSpace Reminder:

Design is not about status. It is about stewardship.

You do not need a Pinterest-perfect home.

You need a space that feels like you.

One light.

One plant.

One prayer.

One moment of beauty.

It is enough.

And now, so are you.

SECTION 09: The SoulSpace Reset Ritual

"Designing a Sacred Weekly Practice"

Healing is not just a one-time realization.

It is a rhythm. A return. A repeated decision to live softer, clearer, more fully at home within yourself.

The SoulSpace Reset Ritual is your anchor practice.

Your ritual to reset your space and your nervous system.

Not in a rush. Not in perfection.

But with devotion.

It is designed to be done weekly, monthly, or anytime you feel disconnected, heavy, or energetically overwhelmed.

This is your spiritual housework.

It is not about cleaning for guests.

It is about preparing your space for yourself.

The 6-Step SoulSpace Reset Ritual:

You can do this in a single morning or spread it out across a slow Sunday.

What matters is presence, not pressure.

Step 1: Clear the Surface, Clear the Energy:

Choose one surface: your nightstand, your coffee table, your altar.

Wipe it down. Remove what does not belong.

As you do, whisper:

"I release what no longer supports me. I open space for what does."

You can also burn sage, rosemary, or simply open a window while you clean.

Step 2: Reset the Senses:

Focus on the five senses:

Add a new texture (fresh linen, a blanket, or natural fiber).

Diffuse essential oils (lavender for calm, citrus for energy).

Play music that softens the atmosphere.

Light a candle that smells like memory or mood.

Bring water into the room; symbol of flow, clearing, baptism.

This awakens the body and re-tunes your home's vibration.

Step 3: Reclaim One Forgotten Corner:

Pick one area you have been avoiding: under the sink, that drawer, the back of your closet.

Do not attack it. Bless it.

Ask:

"What energy has this corner been holding for me?"

Then reset it.

Even if all you do is reorganize it and add a note that says: "You matter."

Step 4: Place Beauty with Intention:

Choose one item to elevate, not just decorate.

Move a favorite book into plain sight.

Rearrange a vignette to reflect your current mood.

Add flowers (real or faux) to a neglected space.

Place an affirmation card where your eyes will meet it.

Beauty does not have to be expensive; it just has to be on purpose.

Step 5: Speak the Room Alive:

Walk room to room and speak aloud what each space is now allowed to hold:

"This room holds rest."

"This corner holds clarity."

"This space makes room for joy."

"This home carries peace, not pressure."

Words reset energy. Your voice carries authority. Let your space hear you.

Step 6: Close With Breath or Prayer:

Stand in your home.

Close your eyes.

Place a hand over your heart or on a wall.

Take three deep breaths.

Or pray:

"Let this home reflect the healing I now carry within me. May every room echo peace, every item serve beauty, every day begin with intention."

Optional Add-On: Sacred Reset Sundays

Choose one day a week to repeat this practice in part or in full.

This becomes your ritual of return.

Call it your SoulSpace Sabbath.

Let it reset not just your space, but your entire week.

SECTION 10: The 7-Day SoulSpace Challenge

"Start Small. Shift Everything."

Not ready to overhaul your space all at once?

You do not need to.

You just need to begin.

The 7-Day SoulSpace Challenge is a gentle invitation to step back into yourself, one breath, one corner, one object at a time.

You do not need a big budget.

You do not need perfect timing.

You just need willingness.

In seven small steps, you will start to remember what peace feels like.

Day 1: Clear One Surface:

Choose the surface, your nightstand, a table, your sink counter.

Remove what does not serve.

Wipe it with intention.

Whisper: "I deserve clear space to feel clearly."

Optional: Light a candle or say a prayer over that space once cleared.

Day 2: Choose One Affirmation:

Pick or write a sentence that grounds you.

Try:

"My home is allowed to reflect my healing."

"I am safe here."

"Stillness is sacred."

Write it down. Tape it to your wall. Say it aloud.

Let this sentence follow you all day.

Day 3: Remove One Item Holding Old Energy:

Find one thing you have kept out of guilt, pain, or obligation.

Hold it. Breathe. Then ask:

"Do I still need to carry this?"

If not let it go.

Optional: Donate, burn, or repurpose it as part of a releasing ritual.

Day 4: Add One Healing Texture:

Choose one item that makes your body say "Ahh."

Try:

A soft throw.

A woven basket.

A pillowcase with weight.

Your favorite t-shirt folded near your bed.

Let your nervous system receive comfort through touch.

Day 5: Introduce a Scent That Grounds You:

Add aromatherapy through:

A candle.

A simmer pot (lemon, cinnamon, herbs).

Essential oil in a diffuser.

Scented drawer liner or linen spray.

As you inhale, say:

"Let this space feel new again."

Day 6: Write a Blessing for Your Space:

This can be a prayer, poem, or simple sentence.

Try:

"Let this home reflect love, growth, and rest. Let it echo softness in every corner. May everyone who enters, including me, feel safe here."

Place your words somewhere visible, or tuck them under your pillow.

Day 7: Sit in Silence for 5 Minutes:

Do nothing.

Just sit in your space.

Notice what you feel.

Where your eyes go.

What emotions surface.

Breathe them through.

This moment is the true reset.

The reminder that healing does not have to be loud.

It just has to be real.

After the Challenge...

You may feel clearer.

You may feel emotional.

You may feel nothing, yet.

All are valid.

The work has begun. And you are doing it beautifully.

From here, move into the reset ritual weekly... or revisit this challenge anytime life feels too loud.

Your SoulSpace is never out of reach.

You always have permission to begin again.

SECTION 11: Designing Through Transitions

"How to Hold Space When Life is Breaking and Rebuilding You"

There are moments when your home does not feel like home.

Moments when your space becomes a holding cell,

a reminder of loss,

a reflection of something you cannot even name yet.

Transitions will test you.

Breakups. Grief. Moving. Illness. Separation. Change you did not ask for.

But even then, your space can still hold you.

This chapter is not about making your home pretty.

It is about making it sacred when everything else feels unstable.

Let us talk about how.

01. When You are Grieving:

Grief fogs everything, including your ability to care for your space.

That is okay.

SoulSpace Tips:

Do not clean. Tend. Wipe a surface. Light a candle. Make your bed, not for discipline, but for dignity.

Create a grief corner. A chair with a blanket. A photo. A journal. A place to sit with your sadness.

Add softness: dim lighting, thick textures, warm scents like cedar or vanilla. Your nervous system needs cradle energy.

Permission: You are allowed to leave one room undone. Grief is not a productivity challenge.

02. After a Breakup or Heartbreak:

You shared a space. A bed. A drawer.

Now everything feels like it echoes their absence.

SoulSpace Tips:

Reclaim the bed: New sheets. New scent. A symbolic object on their side of the bed to honor *you.*

Rearrange one piece of furniture, even a chair. This shifts the energy grid and tells your brain: "Things are different now."

Throw away or donate anything that holds pain without purpose. It is okay to keep some memories, but not if they keep you stuck.

Affirmation: "I deserve to feel good in my space again."

03. When You have Moved (Willingly or Not):

Whether you are upgrading or displaced, moving can fracture your identity.

Everything feels unfamiliar. Untethered. Exhausting.

SoulSpace Tips:

Unpack one sacred object first: A book, a candle, an item from your altar. Something that reminds you who you are.

Introduce a familiar scent into the air your nervous system will register it as "home."

Bless the space, even if it is temporary. Walk room to room and speak:

"You're allowed to hold peace here."

04. When You are Rebuilding After Trauma:

Trauma shatters the body's sense of safety, so your home must become your first healing partner.

SoulSpace Tips:

Clear visual noise. Too many objects = too many decisions. Your brain needs simplicity.

Choose calming color palettes: muted greens, taupes, earth tones, pale blues.

Sleep in softness. Weighted blankets. Fuzzy socks. Low light.

Post affirmations near high-trigger areas:

"You are not back there."

"You are safe now."

Design Note: Healing spaces are not about aesthetics. They are about nervous system repair.

05. When You are Becoming Someone New:

Sometimes, the transition is not pain, it is evolution.

New job. New mindset. New season. You feel like someone different, and your home has not caught up yet.

SoulSpace Tips:

Remove anything that reflects an old identity you have outgrown.

Add visuals of who you are becoming: a photo, a color, a quote.

Move your altar or create one for the first time.

Shift one thing every week that reflects your internal change.

Affirmation: "This space evolves with me."

Final Words for Transition Seasons:

If you are in one of these moments, you are not broken. You are becoming.

And your space does not have to be perfect.

It just has to be safe enough to fall apart and build again.

Let it hold your tears.

Let it make room for silence.

Let it witness who you were and protect who you are becoming.

Your home is not just four walls.

It is the altar of your becoming.

SECTION 12: What Now?

"Your Healing Is Just Beginning"

You made it to the final page.

But this is not the end.

This is a shift.

A remembering.

A reclamation.

A soul-deep YES to a life that feels like peace, not performance.

You have cleared space.

You have spoken life.

You have touched the corners of your home that reflect the corners of you.

So now what?

You live it.

You do not have to do it all at once.

You do not have to buy anything new.

You just have to keep choosing presence over perfection.

Softness over survival.

Alignment over aesthetics.

And when it gets hard, because it will come back to this book.

Come back to the corners.

Come back to the breath.

Come back to the blueprint that now lives inside you.

What You Can Do Next:

1. Join the SoulSpace Community

This is a movement, not a moment.

Connect with others who are reclaiming their homes and themselves.

www.evelynwiggins.podia.com

Tag #TheHealingBlueprint to share your journey.

2. Take the Next Step with Me

The Healing Blueprint is just the beginning.

Coming soon: SoulSpace Alchemy™ a full digital course to teach you the deeper layers of sacred interior design.

Ready to go further?

Sign up for early access at www.evelynwiggins.podia.com

3. Gift the Experience:

This book was made to be passed on.

Buy a copy for someone whose space feels heavy.

Print a favorite affirmation and leave it where it can catch someone's breath.

Be the shift.

4. Write Your Own Blueprint:

You have seen how powerful this can be.

Now create your own version:

Your own rituals

Your own affirmations

Your own SoulSpace mood board.

Your own legacy of healing space.

You do not need permission.

You already have it.

Final Blessing:

May your home speak your truth.

May your rooms become refuge.

May your beauty be on purpose.

May you be held, seen, softened, and safe.

And may you never forget:

You are the blueprint.

And the world is better because you are here.

With everything in me,

Evelyn Wiggins

Founder of ENAM Interiors

Creator of SoulSpace™

References & Resources:

The following sources inspired and supported the insights shared in The Healing Blueprint™:

Princeton Neuroscience Institute (2011) – Visual clutter and cognitive load

National Sleep Foundation (2021) – Effects of warm lighting on melatonin

Somatic Experiencing Institute – Sensory-based trauma healing

NASA Clean Air Study (1989) – Air-purifying indoor plants

Harvard Health Publishing – Aromatherapy and emotional response

Journal of Physiological Anthropology (2015) – Indoor plants and stress reduction

British Journal of Psychology (2018) – Texture and emotional regulation

National Institutes of Health (2020) – Scent and limbic system response

Acknowledgments

To God, thank you for the vision, the voice, and the timing.

To my ancestors, thank you for the strength to endure and the creativity to rise.

To every reader who held this book close and whispered, "That's me."

To the Evelyn who did not give up when it got hard, this one's for you.

About the Author

Evelyn Wiggins is the founder of ENAM Interiors and the visionary behind the SoulSpace™ movement. A soulful interior designer, educator, and healing guide, Evelyn helps people reconnect to themselves through intentional design and sacred space practices. Her work blends Afrocentric healing, psychology, faith, and aesthetic wisdom to create rooms that feel like refuge.

Learn more at:

www.evelynwiggins.podia.com

Follow on Threads, Facebook, and beyond: @EvelynWiggins

Stay Connected:

The healing does not end here.

- Join my email list for free rituals, mood boards, and new product drops

- Get your SoulSpace Starter Kit™ when you sign up

- Be the first to access my upcoming digital course SoulSpace Alchemy™

- www.evelynwiggins.podia.com

www.ingramcontent.com/pod-product-compliance
Lightning Source LLC
Chambersburg PA
CBHW071346130626
46556CB00005B/2054